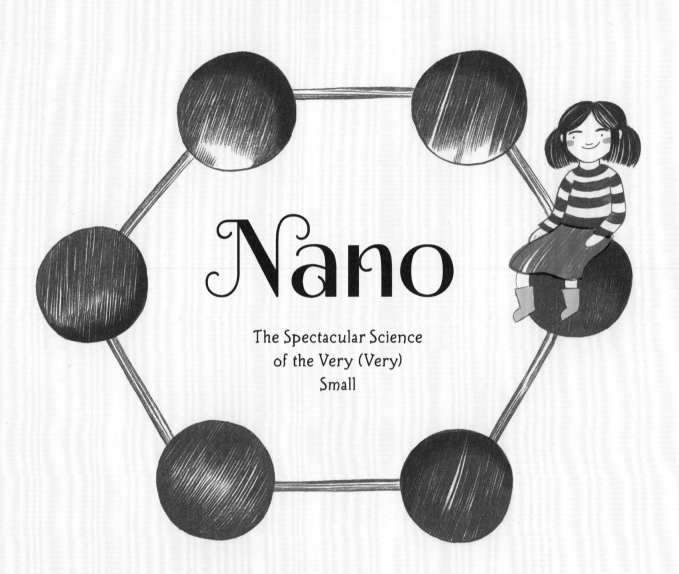

Nano

The Spectacular Science
of the Very (Very)
Small

To my extraordinary family, Charlotte, John, and Charlie, you make my life worth living. And to South Hampstead High School, Dorothy Walgate, and Les Hearn, without whom I would never have become a scientist.
JW

For Helen, the mightiest of humans and the most wonderful friend and agent I could have ever hoped for
MC

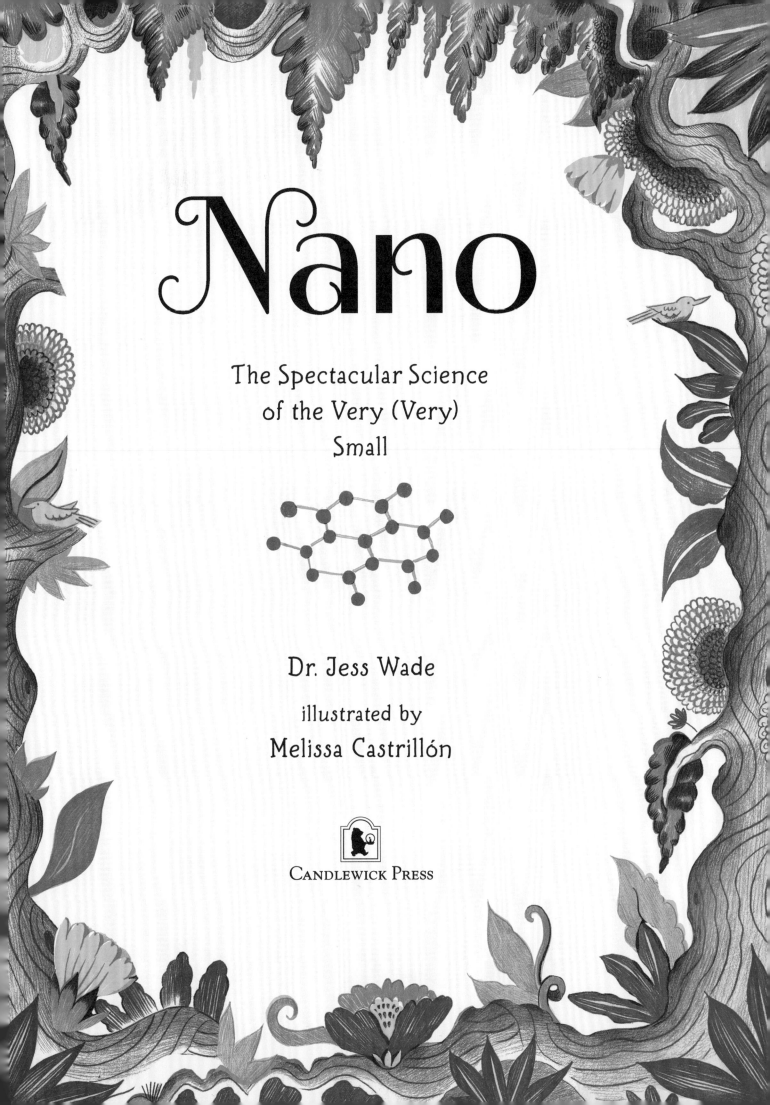

Nano

The Spectacular Science
of the Very (Very)
Small

Dr. Jess Wade

illustrated by

Melissa Castrillón

CANDLEWICK PRESS

Look around your home.
Everything is made out
of *something.*

Paper

Rubber

Glass

Metal

Wood

Cotton

Cardboard

Metal

Glass

Concrete

Cotton

Brick

Wool

Plastic

Glass

Plastic

Stone

Something **light** or something **heavy**,
something **strong** or something **flexible**,
something **smooth** or something **rough** . . .
Each of these "somethings" is perfect for a
different job. Scientists call them **materials**.

This book is made from paper. (Stone would be too **heavy** . . .

and glass would be too **delicate**.)

Imagine a book made of chocolate . . . It would **melt**!

But what makes different materials light, heavy, strong, or flexible?

4

To find out, you need to study them very closely. In fact, you need to look right inside them.

If you did, you would discover that the world is made from tiny* building blocks called **atoms**. Every single thing on this planet is made from atoms.

Stop: read that last sentence again. It's a gigantic idea to get your head around, but it's too important to skip over.

The air you breathe? **Atoms.**

The water you drink? **Atoms.**

Your home and all of your things? **Atoms.**

And each and every living thing, including YOU—

atoms, atoms, **atoms**.

WATER

*"Tiny" doesn't just mean "little"—
it means more than a quintillion
times smaller than a grain of sand.

AIR

MOUNTAIN ROCK

SEA SALT

COTTON

Atoms join one another to form **molecules**. Molecules can be made from just one kind of atom (like oxygen molecules, found in the air we breathe) or from multiple kinds (like water molecules, which are made of hydrogen and oxygen atoms).

KEY:

◯ = HYDROGEN atom

⬤ = OXYGEN atom

⬤ = SODIUM atom

⬤ = CHLORINE atom

⬤ = ALUMINUM atom

⬤ = CARBON atom

—— = a BOND (or a connection between the atoms in a molecule)

There are more than a hundred different kinds of atoms, and each kind is called an element. Some things are made from just one type of element . . .

Coins are often made from nickel.

Fancy pitchers can be made from silver.

Chalk can be made from calcium.

Kitchen foil is made from aluminum.

Cutlery can be made from iron.

The gas in hot-air balloons is helium.

but most are made from several, mixed together.

The way they are mixed together affects how they look and feel— whether they're strong or flexible, light or heavy.

Jewelry can be made from gold, silver, or platinum.

Pencil leads are made from carbon.

This pot is primarily plastic, which is mainly made from carbon and hydrogen.

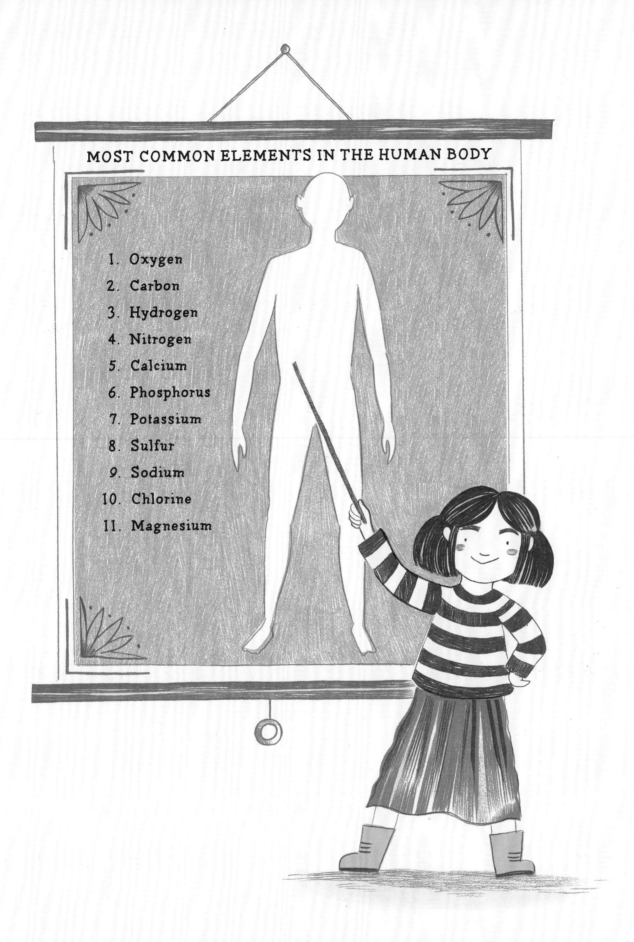

MOST COMMON ELEMENTS IN THE HUMAN BODY

1. Oxygen
2. Carbon
3. Hydrogen
4. Nitrogen
5. Calcium
6. Phosphorus
7. Potassium
8. Sulfur
9. Sodium
10. Chlorine
11. Magnesium

Human beings are made from eleven different elements—including one called carbon. Carbon is a *very* important element.

There's carbon all over the world, in every living thing— from daisies to oak trees, beetles to blue whales.

You can also find carbon on its own in nature. When carbon atoms are arranged in layers, and stacked like playing cards, they make **graphite**.

You probably have some graphite in your schoolbag—it's used to make the lead in your pencils.

Layers of carbon atoms in GRAPHITE

Graphite is soft and smudgy, because the layers of carbon atoms slide over one another—which makes it easy to leave a mark on paper.

Scientists discovered that they could take one layer away from graphite to create a brand-new material, which they called **graphene**.

GRAPHENE

Graphene is so thin that it's see-through, but it's more flexible than rubber and stronger than steel. In fact, it's the strongest material known to human beings.

If you made a tightrope out of graphene, an elephant could walk along it without breaking it.

13

Graphene is a **NANO**MATERIAL—and it's just one atom thick. "Nano" is the word scientists use for anything this tiny.

Because atoms are so very small, scientists have had to build new machines to study them and to move them around.

And even so, it's taken years—and lots of failed experiments—to make materials like graphene.

But it's been worth it, because some nanomaterials are AMAZING!

We're already using graphene to make:

stronger, lighter airplanes that need less fuel to stay in the sky—

which means less pollution in the air . . .

windowpanes that wash themselves using only sunlight . . .

thinner, lighter
phones with
brighter colors . . .

and medicines that doctors
can steer through your
body so that they end up
in exactly the right place.

There's plenty more in store.
Scientists are working to make
sieves with nanosize holes, small
enough to trap even the tiniest
specks of salt and dirt.

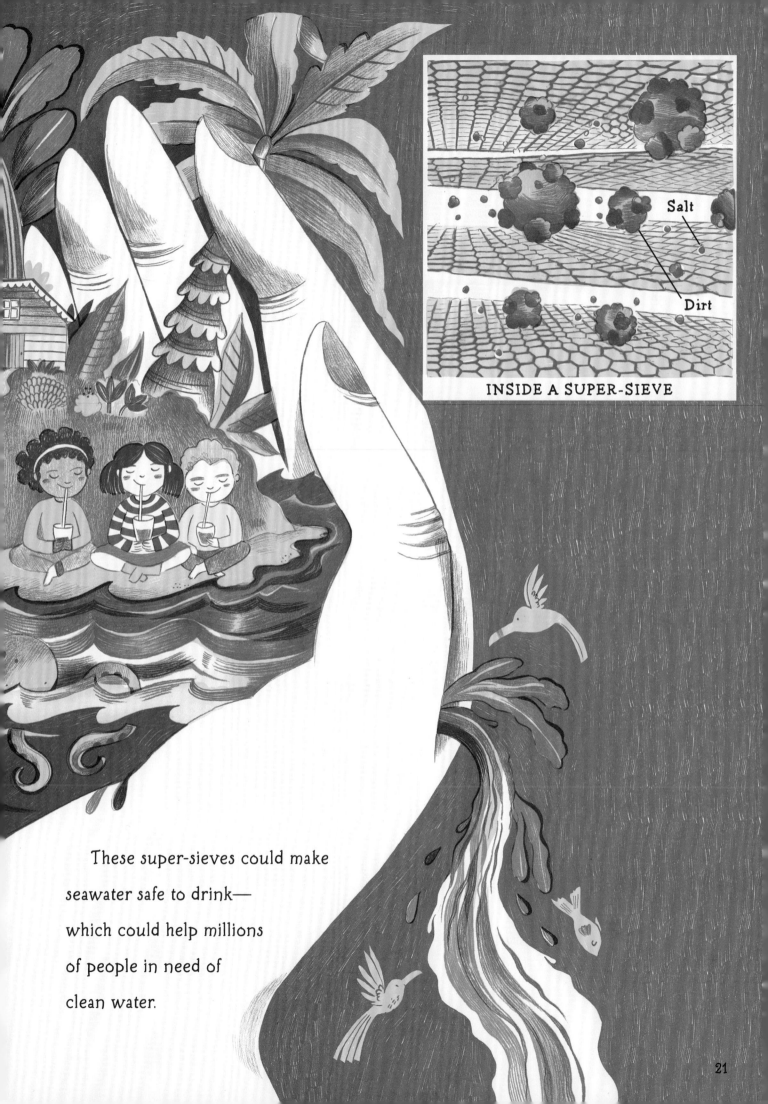

INSIDE A SUPER-SIEVE

Salt

Dirt

These super-sieves could make
seawater safe to drink—
which could help millions
of people in need of
clean water.

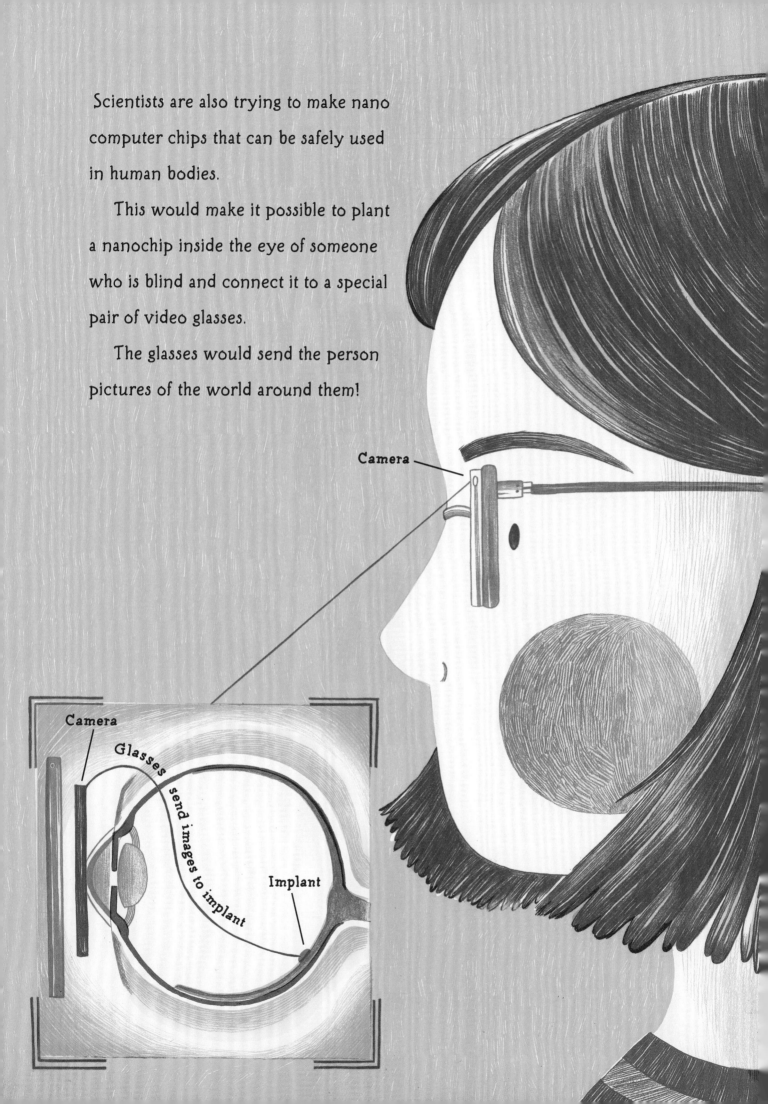

Scientists are also trying to make nano computer chips that can be safely used in human bodies.

This would make it possible to plant a nanochip inside the eye of someone who is blind and connect it to a special pair of video glasses.

The glasses would send the person pictures of the world around them!

Camera

Camera

Glasses send images to implant

Implant

But it takes years
of testing to find out
if new materials are
safe to use—to
be certain they
won't hurt us or
our planet.

Scientists all over
the world are helping to
speed that process along by
sharing advice and new ideas.
As you read this book,
they are conducting experiments,
making some not-so-nano mistakes,
and discovering more about atoms.

24

Nanoscience is a work in progress—and it's going to be the work of years and years to come. There are so many secrets left for scientists to unlock.

And who knows: the person with the key might just be . . .

YOU!

PEANUT B

MORE ABOUT NANOSCIENCE

The first question nanoscientists ask themselves is "What properties do we want our new material to have?"

They might want a material that's tough and strong but also light and flexible; a material that can shine light in a particular color; or a material that's safe to use, in tiny amounts, inside the human body.

Creating, studying, and using nanomaterials require a team of scientists with a whole range of different skills. Once a scientist has decided exactly what they're looking for, it's time to put that team together.

CHEMISTS

The scientists who design and build nanomaterials are **chemists**.

Chemists spend a lot of time researching which elements to use for a new material. They create computer models to explore the many ways in which those elements could form molecules. Once they have an idea they think will work, they begin to plan how to make those molecules in real life.

Perfecting these experiments can take years: scientists have to figure out precisely not only the right quantity of each element to use but also the right temperature, air pressure, and amount of light there should be when they're trying to combine elements.

PHYSICISTS AND ENGINEERS

The scientists who study the different patterns of molecules are usually **physicists** or **engineers**. They examine tiny amounts of new nanomaterials in laboratories called cleanrooms.

Cleanrooms are really, really, REALLY clean: far cleaner than any room in your home or school! They have specially designed filters for trapping even the tiniest specks of dust and dirt, and anything else that might affect new molecules.

Sometimes elements will combine into beautiful shapes and structures without the need for much encouragement. But often scientists have to give them a bit of extra help: for example, by using 3D printers to organize and control the patterns of molecules.

MICROSCOPES

To study the molecules in existing nanomaterials, scientists have designed new kinds of microscopes.

Traditional microscopes aren't useful for nanotechnology, because molecules are so very (very) small. Instead, scientists have built new microscopes with incredibly pointy needles, called **atomic force microscopes**.

Scientists will guide the microscope's needle over the surface of a nanomaterial, and as it meets nanosize mountains and valleys, the point will bounce up and down.

By carefully measuring this bounce, scientists can make a map of the surface, which helps them to identify individual atoms and molecules.

SPECTROSCOPY

To study what molecules are up to inside nanomaterials, nanoscientists can use **spectroscopy**.

Spectroscopy involves shining a super-bright light at a nanomaterial and recording how much light bounces back in each different color of the rainbow.

Scientists can use this to figure out exactly which molecules are inside a nanomaterial and how they're arranged, because every molecule interacts with light in a unique way.

Once they have perfected their nanomaterials, scientists can use them to build the technology you've read about in this book!

INDEX

First US edition 2021

Library of Congress Catalog Card Number 2021946276
ISBN 978-1-5362-1766-7

21 22 23 24 25 26 CCP 10 9 8 7 6 5 4 3

Printed in Shenzhen, Guangdong, China

This book was typeset in Alghera and Arvo.
The illustrations were done in pencil and colored digitally.

Candlewick Press
99 Dover Street
Somerville, Massachusetts 02144

www.candlewick.com